Ritz on Wheels

By Ian Brett

- Preface-

It all started with a desire for freedom and adventure. To be free creates an environment in which your soul and spirit can follow a path of inner contentment. We look to the stars with bewilderment and gaze into the infinity of our world. The need for adventure, however, is held deep within our soul.

That soul escaped on the morning of March 3rd 2021, when upon awakening, my thoughts turned to my now redundant Ford Custom van. She had faithfully served me for 7 years since purchasing her from new and thus, at the age of fifty-six, I, the 'White Van Man' had just retired, bidding farewell to my trusted work companion.

The first sip of black coffee always stirs my senses. With my trusted wife of two decades and more lying next to me, I informed her of our new adventure. "Darling, I am going to convert my now redundant van into a camper van that will endeavour to provide us with a travelling home for the purpose of adventure."

And so, the start of that journey began.

-Acknowledgements-

As ever, I am much indebted to many people for their kind
words and encouragement, which enabled me to bring to fruition
my story.
Gratitude goes to my wife, who has always been there to keep
me grounded and provided me with an environment to flourish.

Special thanks to my daughter for not only being a teacher to
children by profession, but helping me with my grammar and
spelling!

To my son for his support and encouragement.

Antony Redmile for his innovative mind, which is fearless with
no boundaries, has inspired me that anything is possible when
architectural license is applied.

And finally to the many people who have inspired me on my life
journey, I thank you.

- Chapter One -

Walking from my back door to my eagerly awaiting project filled me with a kind of fear that didn't create an environment in which I could flourish. An adventure has to start with that first step, and for me, that first step was into the unknown. My thoughts turned to the first day when I picked up the keys to my new van, which from this day forward will now be known as 'my companion'.

Seven years previous, the adventure unbeknown to me was to start in the form of a new van, a week-long holiday with nowhere to go! Little did I know what lay ahead!

As I drove home in the evening rush hour traffic, a plan began to take shape in my mind. It dawned on me that touring Scotland for seven days, sleeping and living among the clans of the north, was becoming increasingly appealing with every yard gained in that stagnant traffic. So, I decided to make a detour to a builder's merchant to purchase some materials for a bed. With a sense of realism, I pulled up at home with my new plan.

Life in itself is a better journey when your partner can become involved on your adventure. Together, we built our home for our trip from East Scotland to West.

Being a property developer enabled me to develop carpentry skills. I assembled a 3-foot bed at the back behind the cab raising it to allow plastic storage boxes to fit underneath for clothes and food. We packed deckchairs a gas stove and a toilet bucket with a lid and set off on our first trip. Soon other trips followed as we toured France and Spain with us living out of the back of our companion. This giving us the taste for future trips into the unknown.

Early prototype: A trip to Scotland.

Early Prototype: Second class luxury.

- Chapter Two -

Confidence, filled by enthusiasm, filled the morning air as my thoughts gathered. I told myself, "You can do this," as I clicked the key to my new world for 12 weeks.

When I opened my back doors, the epicentre of my working life stared back at me. The honest tools that had become my friends looked worn and well-used as I began to move them to their new home - my workshop. I quickly dismantled the existing raised bed that had served us so well, and cleared all remaining items, including the dust. Henry, my trusted aide, hoovered up the last specks and particles of my previous life, leaving me with a blank canvas to plan and build for our next adventure. What a journey it would become - a journey of finding that anything is possible if you have the clarity that comes from engaging the human brain with knowledge gained from experience and YouTube. Then a whole new world becomes unlocked.

Looking at and researching internal layouts is the catalyst for producing the best layout and fundamentals for your needs. The small space of 8ft x 4ft 9inch is quite a challenge, not only for you, but also for your partner in crime. Thereby, the endless research and measuring to accomplish our Ritz on wheels had begun.

The 'Splitty' or split-window model Volkswagen camper van was released in 1949 and is still one of the most sought-after and popular models to this day. Various new versions, competing with the relics of the past, provide endless opportunities for people of all ages to roam freely around the world.

The opportunity to witness the beauty and craftsmanship of our heritage came when my parents purchased a 1975 VW camper van in which they toured Cornwall. Their adventures resonated with me, and I began to fashion my own ideas to create a layout that was unlike the early camper vans - a layout that combined luxury and practicality.

George Clarke's Amazing Spaces became a must-watch TV program for me. The ingenuity and craftsmanship showcased in the show enlightened me and emphasised that small areas can become big spaces if every inch is utilised and planned for. Innovation is the key.

First and foremost, learning from past experiences, I wanted to create a comfortable bed, not the typical rock and roll generic one most VW camper-vans tend to come with. These beds are usually quite hard and require a foam topper for optimal comfort. However, the upside of this design is that seatbelts can accommodate two extra passengers during transit. Since I had no desire to cater for extra passengers in my design, I was content with being able to carry two passengers plus the driver across the three front berths.

This was a good starting point, as sleep is the gateway to life. I had a blank canvas to work upon. I decided to create an indicative budget, with 5k being the upper limit. I hoped this would be a round sum to work towards. My time was free, but the payment would be the finished article. I would be paid back in adventure.

The Blank Canvas

-Chapter Three -

"Where to start?" became the question of the day. A cup of tea and a Tunnock chocolate bar became the place I levitated to when pondering. As stated in the dictionary, to ponder means to think about something carefully, especially before making a decision or reaching a conclusion. I hasten to add that a lot of tea and Tunnock bars were consumed in copious amounts!

I was, for lack of a better word, overwhelmed. I needed to make decisions, but I feared that these decisions could be costly and wrong. So, I closed the doors and walked away, thinking, "Have I bitten off more than I can chew? Why does the human brain always sow seeds of doubt? Is it a coping procedure we have to go through to get to where we want to be?"

If you ever find yourself in a moment of complete understanding of the circumstances that have led you to your "here and now," everything around you will become still and in sync. Your past, present, and future will converge in a single moment, and all the confusion of your existence will become clear. In this moment of clarity, you will feel empowered to move ahead. The answer is simple: start at the beginning, and everything will fall into place.

I spent the afternoon watching videos on YouTube, learning about various aspects of van conversion, from cutting out windows to electrical and plumbing work. The amount of information and knowledge available is immense. However, the downside is that each video can be subjective, which can lead to doubts about my ability to carry out certain procedures. The only barrier in this case is my self-confidence and trust in my own abilities. These qualities have served me well in my business life as a property developer. Therefore, I made the decision to go ahead with the project, with the understanding that building something in the context of a van is not too different from building in other contexts.

Given the limited space in the van, I realised that swivelling the front bench seats around would provide extra space and make a big difference. With this in mind, I removed the bulkhead divide, which separates the cab and cargo area. The aesthetic improvement was remarkable, and it became apparent that there were no arguments against removing the bulkhead. This boosted my confidence in my initial decision and

motivated me to continue with the project, without any
thoughts of taking on more than I can handle.

Double swiveled seat approved by our German Shepherd, Piper.

As my head hit the pillow each night, my thoughts were always
geared towards the tasks ahead or reflecting on the
achievements of the day. I became unknowingly consumed by the
van conversion, and it became a regular occurrence to wake up
full of ideas. This pattern continued for the duration of the
12 weeks (84 days) of the project. It felt like climbing a
staircase to a summit, with each step becoming tangible as I
touched and moulded every inch and space of the van.

The excitement grew as I awaited the call informing me that my
new opening side window was ready to be fitted. I decided to
have only one window behind the driver's seat, as on our past
trips, we had no windows at all. Having one opening window
seemed reasonable. I chose not to undertake the drilling and
cutting out of the side aperture myself, as it seemed like a
task beyond my capabilities. This decision was justified when
the window was fitted and transformed the look of the van from
both the inside and the outside. The dark black smoked glass
gave a sleek appearance and made the interior brighter. I

found myself gazing out, visualising the endless views that would surround me. The team that fitted the window did a perfect job, and upon payment, they smiled at each other and jokingly said, "I bet you contact us to put a window on the other side!" How right they were!

Every day, packages would arrive, containing the items I ordered. The first item was the bitumen-backed silver sound-deadening material. I removed all the internal side ply linings, revealing the bare structure of the van. I proceeded to stick the sound-deadening material to all the flat panels and wheel arches, covering the centre portion of the van's panels. This material helps reduce road noise and the droning sound of traffic. It makes the van feel less hollow when tapping the outside structure. Instead of a tinny sound, you only hear a dull thud.

I was conscious that all aspects of our conversion had to be built and constructed to a high standard. I already had vast experience in turning out a product where the bar for standards was always high. This standard had to apply to every task and procedure. It always helps when time isn't of the essence, but the ability to be self-critical would play devil's advocate with oneself. The little man on one shoulder would say, "that's okay," only for the same man on the other shoulder to sow the seed of doubt. Hence, the latter always became triumphant. This scenario would always play out!

- Chapter Four -

I am now having conversations and pleasantries with our post person. A prerequisite of a conversion should be to take out shares in Royal Mail. What a great institution Royal Mail is, and their people are delivering in all weathers. Since online ordering has become popular, the days of just delivering letters are consigned to history. I duly rewarded our post person with a humble gift at Christmas.

The Aborigines, the indigenous people of Australia, existed in their own world. They lived in the moment, having no concept of time or thought process of yesterday or tomorrow. I began to live this existence. Time became irrelevant. Transfixed in my workshop with my radio, as time passed, my focus became measured. It was as if I had been given an opportunity, and someone else was directing this opportunity. I began not to ponder as much, but to let my creative being evolve.

Keeping out the cold and creating a barrier between ourselves and Mother Nature has over time evolved into a billion-pound industry. Thermal cavities hold back the sub-zero elements using all kinds of materials. I researched and obtained a recycled wool type insulation made from old bottles and their tops. The upside of using such material is reduced condensation. So, I stuffed and placed this material into every nook and cranny, making sure not to over pack it, as air trapped within provides a warmer air pocket. You could tell that a thermal barrier had been created, as putting your face up close gave warmth and a sense that the insulation was doing its job.

I then purchased a roll of silver solar bay self-adhesive thermal foil insulation, 15mm thick. This has superior thermal properties, not only to retain heat within the van but also to reflect the sun away. We had, in all senses and purposes, created a thermal barrier against the world, and the internal space became to resemble a spaceship with all elevations shimmering silver with the light that resonated through our new window.

The transformation and the newness of my new capsule became a stark contrast from the place it had evolved from. My gaze became transfixed on the part of my rear sliding door where I now could envisage a window to match with the other side. I duly laughed to myself that the team that had fitted the previous one were right in their observation that they would be returning, and return they did. The old adage of "I told

you so" was played out by them, but the humble pie I had to
eat was a testament to the fact that it's not the mistake that
has been made, but the nature in which you acknowledge and
correct that mistake.

Yet again, the team carried out a first-class job, but upon
payment, they laughed at each other again. With the art form
of a double act, they informed me that they might be returning
to place windows in the rear top quarters of the rear doors.
They even jokingly locked me in their van, as they had rear
windows to validate their opinion that it would finish and
enhance my van. I duly declined their kind concern and became
somewhat respectful of their business and sales model. I
wondered what percentage of work procurement was gained by
playing out this scenario. I waved them on their way and hoped
I wouldn't have to eat a double dose of humble pie!

I hasten to add that the look and transformation were
magnificent, and the retro-fit design enhanced and
complemented my companion.

**The now cut out windows and gallery
kitchen taking place.**

– Chapter Five –

The gallery was to be my favoured layout design, producing a narrow walkway from front to back with a right turn to the side door. I drew a line onto the floor to place the alleyway slightly off-centre, allowing for 600mm for our concertina bed. This ingenious design of a settee in the day, pulling out over the alley to create a 1200mm (4ft) bed at night. The product was bought on eBay, and upon coming across this, I decided to build the whole design around this bed. I included drop-down doors at the front, allowing spacious storage underneath.

As for mattresses, that was an area I needed to explore. Having owned two caravans in the past, I always found the mattresses not conducive to a good night's sleep. Foam is normally the choice for these mattresses, so I found 2 no 600mm (2ft) wide x 1800mm (6ft) long sprung memory foam quality mattresses and duly placed my order. So, in the daytime, one mattress became the back of the settee, with the other serving as the base, pulling out to form a queen bed.

 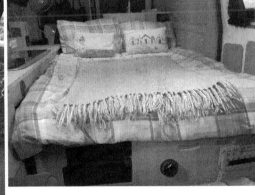

The settee by day; Double bed by night.

Planning electrics and 12V battery supply was something I was looking forward to. I had, from the age of 15, been somewhat interested in electrics and their workings. However, with the recession in full swing and Mrs. Thatcher at the head of the government, jobs, particularly apprenticeships, were in short supply. Not for the want of trying, I wrote to over 20 electrical companies in Leicestershire and only got 1 interview. This, however, was a time when, if you didn't stay on at school, beggars can't be choosers. You had to take what jobs were on offer. So, I secured a bricklaying apprenticeship and duly passed with distinction.

I would always be up to the challenge of repairing any problems with my first cars, be it mechanical or electrical. I was guided by the Haynes manuals of their day. (Yes, we all had to purchase a Haynes car manual.) These were the go-to help books, detailing every aspect of a car's mechanics and workings, with a full breakdown of how to replace and renew every part of a vehicle. They were brilliant books for their era and were often given as Christmas presents for the discerning new car owner.

The main van battery is housed under the driver's seat. I began to explore the possibility of siting the 12V leisure battery next to it, but this looked to be very tight and difficult to access. So, I placed the leisure battery behind the driver's seat. I purchased this from Halfords, as I have always found their batteries to be good value. And if they become faulty within their guarantee period, they have always exchanged it for a new one. My thinking was that if my leisure battery was to play up, you are never too far from a Halfords in Britain. I hope this theory is never put to the test!

The idea and practice of a leisure battery is that you can become self-sufficient living off-grid. The 12v system becomes charged by various methods. A split relay charger kit is an electrical arrangement that safely charges the secondary leisure battery of a vehicle. It protects the starter battery by isolating it from the leisure battery when the engine is off and resumes charging only when the engine is running. This ensures that there is no chance of your main battery becoming drained. It will only charge the leisure battery when the main battery is full.

I fitted this split relay charger to my leisure battery and turned on the engine. After a couple of minutes, I heard a click and the red dot light on the relay panel came on, indicating that my leisure battery was being topped up with a charge!

Solar panels can also be fitted to top up your leisure battery. However, I decided that I could always revisit this later if I needed to.

I purchased an on-board battery charger, which automatically keeps your battery topped up when you are on mains hook up (240v). This method and the split relay charging system are the two I implemented.

Now that the battery was in place, I started to plan the 12v system. The list of electrical items includes a TV, aerial amplifier, spotlights, fridge, fan, water pump, and USB ports.

I purchased a control panel with an LED light-up voltage gauge built-in. This is an important part of the 12v system as it allows you to always be aware of the charge your battery is holding. I ran all wires to this control panel, which incorporates switches housing fuses for the relevant amps to control and protect the electrical equipment.

The amount of cables needed to facilitate all your electrical needs is by no means an easy feat. Each cable has to be the right size to handle the load of the given equipment, and care

The gallery kitchen.

needs to be taken to ensure this is correct, as most runs of cables become inaccessible once they are behind enclosures.

Since the early type smaller camper vans became fashionable in the 50s and 60s, they have now evolved into high-tech machines in which all modern conveniences can be integrated. Even an old VW can now be retrofitted with all the modern electrical gadgetry, making them real home-from-home multi-purpose vehicles for living in or adventures.

- Chapter Six -

To dare, is to dream. Making that leap from a homeowner or renter to a full-time van lifer is an inroad into the soul of adventure. The choice of lifestyle becomes the reward for taking that leap.

If an Englishman's home is his castle, then a van lifer's home is a castle on wheels. To be able to take your home to various places on this earth, where you can park up freely, is an experience that is unfortunately illegal in some countries. This takes away a liberty that should be enjoyed by everyone. Having the right to choose to become a nomad should be considered a basic human right.

The rise in house prices in 2022 has made it insurmountable for many people to become homeowners. Therefore, an alternative way of living is becoming more appealing to some. Whether it's purchasing a barge or a van, it is good that we have the freedom to make life choices about where and how we live.

The comfortable nature of living in traditional accommodation is often taken for granted. This needs to be replicated to a certain degree in the van life lifestyle.

As I started organising my workshop, it began to resemble a fully-fledged shop. Opened boxes of materials filled every corner as I proceeded to order and commandeer all the necessary stock. Some of the items included a cooker, fridge, toilet, bed mattresses, carpet, wood for furniture, water container, gas locker, gas bottles, TV with bracket, kettle, and a travel table. The exhausting daily intake of parcels continued as I pondered with a cup of tea and a Tunnock bar. I eventually found a space to sit in my workshop with the doors of my van wide open. I gazed into my project with wide-eyed anticipation. If only I had a Harry Potter wand, I could point it at every box and then point it to the exact place where the contents of the box needed to be. The visualisation of my project continued to develop as I indulged in my thoughts. As the saying goes, "A picture paints a thousand words," and the clarity in my brain became apparent.

With this newfound clarity, the urge to fast forward diminished. Although I wanted the finished product here and now, I knew that the satisfaction would not be the same if my dreams were brought into reality instantaneously. Dreams need to be nurtured over time so that the contented satisfaction of turning a dream into reality becomes embedded in the soul forever. Moving forward with a vision is what allows us to create something beautiful. In your mind's eye, beauty is truly in the eyes of the beholder.

As the element of space is advantageous when van-building, my task for today was to fit the front swivel base to the front bench seat. I duly removed the existing bench seat and bolted the new swivel base into place. When replacing and bolting the seat back, it becomes pivotable. The new base comes with a crash test certificate and is undoubtedly a must-have facility. The swivel base has only been available for bigger motorhomes and VW vans, but a company has just started manufacturing them to retrofit a Ford Custom van, and I was one of the first to obtain one. The only drawback to adding the swivel base is that it raises the front bench seat by 50mm, but this is a small price to pay for the luxury of swivelling the front double seat around.

Front cab seats swivelled round into living area.

I started to look at other elements of retrofitting as new concepts began to evolve for the Ford Custom van. Pop-top conversions are a great addition; it involves cutting out the van roof and fitting strut hinges to allow for extra headroom. Also, a bedroom can be incorporated into this design with a small ladder to access. In itself, it is a great enhancement for families, with the added benefit of extra sleeping accommodation. But on reflecting, I decided not to proceed with a pop top. I reasoned that my factory-fitted roof rack, which folded flat when not in use, was more valuable to me as I could carry my 2 kayaks and transport them.

It has become apparent that I was, by and large, constructing a bespoke conversion, which would become a one-of-a-kind version. I am grateful to the many people who had turned their heads and hands into manufacturing bespoke fittings and concluded that the timing of my project was, in fact, at the forefront of cutting-edge development of ingenious design ideas.

- Chapter Seven-

Paying for a van is without a doubt going to be conducive to your budget, whether you pay £2k or £30k for a van. This is going to be your build, so be bold and inventive. There is no right way, only your way.

The feeling you get when you book that next trip is inner contentment to get in that zone of hitting the open road is like a drug. I, for one, do not sleep well the night before as the next adventure is only hours away, and the excitement of packing and cramming every item and essentials into every space becomes
a work of art in which I take great pride. You are, in essence, moving your home into a smaller version. This is what makes van life an adventure in itself.

To give my companion that homely feel, I decided that I would carpet all elevations. I already had the ply panels, which I removed, and I purchased a ply lining for the ceiling. I chose a light grey four-way stretch carpet, and the contact adhesive spray glue arrived, so I set out to apply the first carpet to a panel. The contact adhesive became a permanent fixture on my fingertips over the course of a week. It would be like growing an extra layer of skin, but moulding the 4-way stretch carpet to the panels gave a transformation and decorative feel, and on completion, it looked amazing. I indeed enjoyed carrying out

The four-way
stretched
carpet taking
shape.

this task, but the enjoyment became short-lived as I tackled
the inner struts between the panels. This, in itself, was
tricky, as the 4-way carpet had to be moulded in 4 ways. With
a bit of trial and error, I quickly mastered the task at hand,
and the van took on its new decorative status.

The first trip was going to be the window of opportunity into
the wonderland of van life. I had never experienced the luxury
aspect of holidaying in style, only the endurance of a basic
conversion in which the basic principles are in place. But to
have the vision of this concept lets the imagination run into
overdrive. I already now had the carpeted interior with the
slick-looking lining in place. I now had to start the fitting
out which would take my companion to the next level.

I had the privilege of learning about the concept of
architectural licence from the flamboyant and eccentric London
designer, Anthony Redmile. His designs and visions in the
1960s and 1970s garnered a loyal following. Antony's mind was
a creative labyrinth, filled with a flair for the unusual.
Having worked alongside this master of creativity, I became
intrigued and inspired to implement my own architectural
licence. This involved thinking outside the box and working
towards creating a masterpiece.

I soon realised that my dream was becoming a reality. The core of my spirit is a passion for adventure, and these adventures create an ever-changing horizon. This horizon was now within my grasp. Armed with knowledge from research, I moved on to the fit-out of my van.

I favoured a gallery layout for the van, which I drew on the floor. Various items, such as a leisure battery, WC, fridge, gas hob, sink, water storage, TV, and gas locker, needed to be built along the right-hand side, behind the driver's seat. Additionally, the area needed to provide worktop space. Incorporating all these items into a 2.5m run posed a challenge but was a workable concept.

I selected a light oak melamine from B&Q and began constructing cupboards and housings. The WC unit needed to resemble a normal unit but discreetly house the WC. I added a lift-up lid attached by a gas strut and hinged at the front. This lid was removable, providing access to the battery and on-board charger located underneath.

With all the electrics in place, the focal point of the living
accommodation became a visual masterpiece within the galley of
units. The worktop, running the length of the van, housed
numerous essentials. The first unit housed the leisure
battery, consumer unit, and charger. Above that, the WC was
placed. The second unit contained the fridge, and the third
unit housed the gas hob and sink. Doors provided storage space
for a water container, with a pump that would pump water to a
small hinged tap that folded into the sink unit. This unit
also had a glass hinged top, which provided extra worktop
space when not in use. A hole in the floor served as a waste
outlet. The final unit was the gas locker, a metal unit with a
built-in drop vent in the floor. As gas is heavier than air,
any leakage would escape through the vent hole in the floor.
The gas locker door was lockable and had a built-in seal.
Achieving smart ingenuity within such a small space was a
testament to meticulous planning during the design stage.

The inaugural trip with this new concept involved leaving the comforts of home for a smaller version of it. We headed to a campsite in Snettisham Beach, Norfolk. This small, un-spoilt seaside resort, divided by a main road, is nestled next to one of the Queen's residences, Sandringham Estate. On the other side of the main road, down a one-mile track road, is Snettisham Beach Resort. Here, a yacht club stands at the end of the wash, a tidal estuary where waves lap along the sand shingle beach. Shanty dwellings, some converted into luxury holiday homes, create a backdrop, while neighbouring homes still favour the beach shack look and vibe.

The vibe of this place entices a crowd of people who return for its unique experiences. Behind the dwellings and static caravans lies a saltwater lagoon, where I have enjoyed kayaking on occasions. It also provides a facility for yacht master training when the sea tide is far removed from the shores of Hunstanton.

We British are always at one with the weather, adapting to the seasons and embracing our climate. Whether the sun is shining or the wind is blowing, it becomes the norm for us. However, on May 15, 2021, with the rain and wind biting deep, we sought shelter in the comfort of our van.

On closing the sliding door, we retreated into our new world. I had already set up our home for 2 nights, with the front seat swivelled around and electric hooked up to mains voltage. The thermal blackout covers were fitted to all cab windows, creating a cosy and homely feel. And so, our first trip away commenced with the onus being to fact-find and iron out all relevant problems, making sure future trips became more comfortable.

I had mounted our 24-inch TV to the side panel of the van, above the worktop, and purchased a TV aerial which I could stick on the outside. This gave us a directional signal, regardless of our position. Our aerial was then amplified by a 12V signal booster, making it possible to obtain terrestrial TV in most locations. Our TV had an integrated DVD player, which proved invaluable on rare occasions when a signal was not possible. We all love a movie night, so maybe I had better start packing some popcorn!

With a glass of red wine in hand, taking in my surroundings, I became somewhat emotional. Not emotional in the sense of being upset, but in that I had created something of outstanding beauty. I had not had the time to reflect on my achievements, so now, sitting in my captain's chair, which was to become my seat of choice, my view from this advantageous point gave me a narrow panoramic view. And as I gazed with inner contentment around my companion, an inner contentment filled my being as the red wine engulfed my soul.

With our first trip complete, we set off on our journey home. Armed with knowledge from our trip, we tasked ourselves with the question: did everything work okay as planned, or did we need to tweak anything? The cab of our companion fell silent as we looked at each other and awaited for one of us to speak. Nothing. We could only speak positively about all our experiences, and everything we designed and installed had worked perfectly. Was this a detriment to our abilities to foresee every aspect of design and workability? I would like to suggest it was. But sometimes in life, you are guided subconsciously, which plays a part in shaping the outcome.

Wardrobe at rear

Chapter Eight

Having now developed a taste for adventure, our next trip took us to Castleton in the Peak District. This was our first off-grid trip, relying on our 12-volt system. We quickly realised that heating would be an issue as the cold set in very quickly at the high altitude of the Peak District. Fortunately, our saving grace was our gas ring, which ensured we remained warm until bedtime. However, after five minutes with the gas on full and the window slightly open, I soon discovered that condensation built up within the van. This method of providing heat would not be ideal, so I would need to come up with an alternative. This was the first problem that had arisen, and my mind would be taxed with finding an alternative off-grid method to provide a heat source.

The Peak District, set in rural Derbyshire, is exquisite in its outstanding beauty. With rolling countryside and lofty mountains, your gaze is always held as you take in the panoramic scenery. This area is known as one of our 15 national parks, and I, for one, will be returning to explore further.

Every lorry with a sleeping compartment cab is fitted with a diesel heater. These small devices, no bigger than a 2-litre coke bottle, provide a heat source within a confined space. I tasked myself with finding and fitting my own heat source.

I engaged myself with more tutorials and armed with this knowledge, I ordered the relevant parts and began the installation process. The diesel heaters can be fuelled directly from your vehicle's fuel tank, or an auxiliary tank can be added. However, finding space in my already fitted-out van became difficult. Therefore, I felt the best way to save space would be to draw fuel from my main fuel tank.

I drove my van onto the ramps, which I carry with me to level the living space, and went about unbolting the main fuel tank and lowering it clear of the under chassis. This was made easier by the fact that I had run the tank down, so minimal diesel was left, making the tank lighter.

By default, the tank has a small nipple positioned on top which I duly sliced with a sharp knife and inserted a straw and a cap which after 2 clicks fitted over this nipple, enabling the diesel heater to draw fuel from my main tank. I reattached the tank back into position and went about installing the heater, which had to be placed under the bed on the opening cargo door side.

For all the pipe work to reach the heater, a 5-inch hole had to be cut into the main van floor. I purchased a hole saw and, after much deliberation, I managed to find the perfect place to cut out this hole and fixed everything together as per the instructions. The heater is now fixed into position, and with a display panel mounted on the inside wall, I switched the on button to start up.

The heater in position under bed on the opening cargo door side.

I was overjoyed as, within 2 minutes, heat started to come out of the vent and the thermostat read 21 degrees. I had overcome the problem I encountered in the Peak District, and now I had my off-grid heat source, which was to prove invaluable.

The budget I had set myself of £5k had now been compromised, but as I found, everything that is small comes at a cost. I did not want to compromise any aspect of my journey into the unknown, and my embryonic status as a bespoke designer left me with the desire to finish my project. The finishing touch to the aesthetic look had to be four top-of-the-range tyres to complete my now ritzy on wheels.

My journey into the unknown taught me that anything in life is possible. Working outside your comfort zone produces an environment in which learning can only be achieved through spirited research and hard work. Yes, you can take shortcuts, but that journey would be compromised. You have to learn to fail before you can enjoy success, and I feel that epitomised my adventure.

My journey had not ended; it was just about to start...

Printed in Great Britain
by Amazon

32225483R00018